BREAKABLE THINGS

KATIE WISMER

poetry & prose

for anyone who needs a second chance
or a fresh start
even if you don't know what that looks like yet

and for Benny
how lucky I am to have loved you

also by katie wismer

contents

i. the good things

sometimes
the good things
aren't good at all

it's just today

it's watching my cat sleep
and drinking water
when I'm thirsty
and dancing around to the same song
a hundred times

it's remembering a time
when it was so hard
to feel happy

and now
it doesn't take much
of anything at all

I keep telling myself
if I have enough good things
the bad ones can't hurt as much

time has been slipping away
swept out by the current
until I can't see the moments
enough to remember them anymore

and if I think too much about it
it feels like a tragedy
to lose that little girl
with purple glasses
and green crocs
posing on the porch
for her first day of school

but as the waves of my life
ebb and flow

as I watch my face mature
into my mother's

as my parents' lives
morph and adjust
to a new version
without me in it

I realize now
when I go back to visit
I can laugh with them
about jokes I never used
to understand

I recognize
the light in their faces
as they have the time
to follow their own dreams again

and now
instead of rolling my eyes
as they share stories
of when they were young

I collect them all
like the breakable things
they are

and tuck them away
in the safest places
I can find

<u>things the sickness hasn't taken</u>

the way I feel some songs
down to every nerve in my body
and can't help but dance like a fool

the jump I do to get out of bed
at three in the morning
when I have an idea
I don't want to forget

the way she says *I love you*
and I know she means it
even if she can't remember why

but I wish I could remember more

I like rewatching movies
I've seen a million times
finding comfort
in knowing how it will end

then I can go back to the beginning
before characters died
before things changed
and it makes me feel
like the past isn't lost

that every moment
no matter how distant
is frozen in time
untouched and exact

even if I can't quite find
my way back to it

the old me
has been gone
for a while

her memory
is grainy
and black and white

a movie of a past life
so distant from this one

the new me
is blurry
backlit by the sun

inching closer
but still not here

and this version
now

is caught between
the strings they both hold

suspended
and waiting
with sleepless nights
and bated breath

just a shell
waiting for its owner
to return

if success is a rattlesnake
then happiness is a carnival ticket

love is an accessory

honesty is the color of a sweater
you wash time and time again

fading so slowly
you don't notice
the gradual change
over time
until it's so worn
you have to replace it

I've found
I prefer the quiet success
over the
glamorized imposter

the peace of waking up each day
able to stretch my body
and my mind

to let the creativity overflow
and run down my fingertips

without worrying about

where it will land
or if some valuable piece
will slip away

are you really happy
if there's no one to tell

are you really succeeding
if there's no one to watch

are you really living
if you have to think that way

I've never been one for gardening
I don't like the dirt
under my fingernails

but I've always loved flowers
so much so
I've never been able to choose a favorite

it's so easy to fall in love
with the end product
but be unwilling to take on
the journey

there are few things in your life
for which you'd endure the process
a hundred times over

with writing
I love it all

the days it's flowing so well
my fingertips can't keep up

the days the ink runs dry
and I'm left staring at blank pages

the naysayers and negative reviews
the waiting game
and constant doubt

so even if my days are numbered
and my success is past
if all I have left
are half-finished poems

it would still be enough

that is my hope for you

you deserve more
than just a fleeting love of flowers

you deserve a fire
that goes beyond
smiling at pretty things

but I hope you buy yourself the flowers too

I wonder if all the people
I've loved silently
could feel it somehow

maybe they didn't know
where it was coming from

maybe they didn't know
it was me

but for a time
everything in their life
just felt a bit easier
a little less heavy

could they feel
some more good fortune
in the universe for them
just for a little while

I love the peace I feel
when I think of those
who have harmed me

because I've given them
the forgiveness
they never asked for
and will likely never deserve

but my healing
has never been
about them

I no longer feel sorry for myself
over the pain inflicted

I feel sorry for them

because I've shed myself
of their darkness
but they've lost
my light

I do believe the universe
has a way of removing
people who are a detriment
to your life
if you don't do it yourself

there are some shades of pain
I've decided I'd rather endure
than live without

like the anxiety
that plants seeds
under my skin
but I just keep watering it
with caffeine

how foolish it must seem
to be unwilling to let go
of such small things

but I don't think
we get to decide
what brings us peace

how lucky I am
for this life I live

how lucky I am
to spend it with myself

I'm so grateful to have a human body, a human experience. this body feels so much joy, so much pleasure. tasting my favorite foods. feeling a deep stretch. seeing paw prints in the snow. the sunlight coming through the trees. the moon in the sky during the day. a sunset that paints the walls of my apartment red. fresh air in my lungs. when a stranger smiles at you and you can see how genuine it is in their eyes. feeling butterflies in your stomach. to be completely struck with awe. pure joy watching my cats. listening to music and ASMR and meditating and dancing and laughing and singing and smiling and crying and shouting.

I have such a beautiful life.

and I forgive myself for not waking up to it sooner.

it's a fragile kind of hope
delicate

that we missed our chance
the first go around

but there's still time now

I wasn't ready for you then
my life needed to shatter
so I could piece myself back together

I don't believe in fate
or right timing

and maybe it's hopeless
to keep holding on to you

but even after all of our years apart

I've always thought
one day we'd work it out

if you let me go
a second time
I guess I'll have my answer

you are sitting in the shade
on a summer day

a startling laugh
when I can't stop crying

lying drunk on the couch
curled by the fire

and I know you'll smile
and roll your eyes
if you ever read this poem

but

you are everything
that makes me feel safe
after a life spent
looking over my shoulder

you are everything
that makes sense
after years
of stumbling in the dark

you didn't come into my life quickly
not the first time I saw you

it must have been weeks
months
before we ever exchanged words

I don't remember the day
I learned your name

I don't remember the moment
you became important to me

maybe that's why
you sunk in so deep

a little bit
at a time

instead of all at once

the light outside my window
is always too bright at night
on days after it snows

I've never invested in curtains
so I open the blinds
and watch the sun rise

now that you've started staying over
you've noticed it too
and we both can't sleep

but the light looks so different now
falling on you
instead of an empty side of the bed

I know you love the snow
and I never have

now I just don't mind as much

it's a hum
like fingertips
down my spine
the vibrations
inviting themselves
into my veins

and it's just

singing in the shower
or bobbing your head
to a song
only you can hear
while you cook breakfast

but also

it's the way
I love you tastes
in my mouth
after a glass of wine

as the sun slants
through the kitchen window
and your socks skate
across the polished floor

you are somehow
a child so full of glee

it's like you've never
been broken by the world

and yet

you are also
the only man
who looked hell in the face
after breaking the lock in my chest

and you didn't even blink

what memory comes to mind first
when you hear my name?

perhaps not a memory

what feeling?
what word?

because I hear yours
and I close my eyes and smile

my heart slows
like I just got home

and I remember
the night we drank so much
we couldn't walk
without pressing our arms together

and sitting in the trunk of your car
in a pretty dress
afterwards
laughing as we tried to count the stars

whatever you think of
I just hope it's something good

I like the way you smile
beneath my hands on your face

and if trust had a color
it would be the green of your eyes
or maybe the warmth
of your breath on my neck

didn't anyone ever tell you
girls like me
don't come with guarantees

but now you call me baby
and I call you when I walk home

and you ride the train early
in yesterday's clothes

so when I see them
and it makes me feel small

I try on the face I learned from you
and it doesn't sting the same

how silly
I must be
to fall in love so easily

how foolish
to catch one glimpse
and be so certain

how resilient
to remain so hopeful
despite the many times
I've been wrong

how much more beautiful
life is
the softer
I've let myself
become

how lovely it is
to be in love with a person
and not an idea

for a while
I thought
feelings like these
this kind of intensity
was lost

folded between the years of my youth
like a flower pressed between
the pages of a book

I'll take the comments about teen angst as a compliment

I finally pried off the boards
shielding the door in my chest
and let everything inside
desperate to breathe
spill out

but the best part of it
was not the outcome
it was the overwhelming relief
strong enough to bring me
to my knees

that I would no longer
have to wonder
what would happen
if I did

ii. the hard things

I always thought
the hard part
would be getting over him

that after I finally purged
his face from my dreams

and stopped hearing his voice
in my favorite song

whatever came next
would be the easy part

but now that my heart
feels mended

and I've stopped looking
for his shadow to appear
around every corner

I miss having someone
so ingrained
in my soul

the hardest part
was not
letting him go

it's wondering

waiting
willing
myself
to feel like that
for someone else

maybe the only reason for him
was the me
who came out of it

a me
I needed to be

maybe life was cruel
to mold me that way
or maybe it had tried
a few other times
and I'd unknowingly resisted

maybe he was just
the last resort

looking back on it
I think he loved me
in whatever way he knew how
and despite everything
I'm still tempted sometimes
to see if he could do it better now

do I create art
out of the pain
or have I been
surrounding myself with pain
because I'm afraid
the art won't stay
without it

I can't help but wonder
if everyone else
has spent their lives
hurt more often than not

all of their hypocrisy
even when undisturbed by me

grows fangs and wings
and reaches new heights
day after day

and you can spend your whole life
toeing the edge of the roof
or jumping from the ledge
with the hope that one day
you'll learn how to fly and catch them

but all you'll ever do
is give them exactly
what they wanted

the opportunity
to watch you fall

I wish
I'd loosened my grip sooner
that I'd learned
to relax my shoulders
before the tension caused
too much damage

to enjoy the way life feels
when your brain isn't quite developed
and the rationalities
feel less absolute

you get rewarded
in the smallest increments
and focusing on the little tasks
makes forgetting the rest of the world
all too easy

they tell you
you're one of the smart ones
but you've only ever looked at
part of the picture

the first eighteen years of my life
are filed away
under glowing report cards
and shiny red letters

and the perfection used to taste

so sharp on my tongue
that I barely know how
to function anymore
without the blood
in my mouth

I cannot remember
the exact moment
I lost it

the day or time
it crept out into the night
bare feet on wooden floor
leaving the door unlocked behind it

I cannot remember
exactly what it felt like
when it was here

maybe something like
a summer breeze
or popsicles by the pool
when we were children

all I know is
what it's like living
without it

how hard it can be
to get out of bed

the pacing around my apartment
I don't realize I do

the vices and desperate prayers at night
to something I don't believe in

is it something we all lose
or did I do something wrong
along the way

the absence of distractions
has brought noise
not quiet
questions
not peace

maybe I've conditioned myself
so I can only love things
that hurt a little

because for some reason
I just can't get enough
of people who think
I'm too much

on the days
when life just
isn't easy
I remind myself
I can do hard things

but then the days
when it's not as heavy
pass by
without me
even noticing

I am overwhelmed
by how underwhelmed I feel
so much of the time

I'm more plugged in
than I've ever been
and also the most
out of touch

overstimulated
and under appreciated

so swept up
in the lives around me
it's like some kind
of crutch

maybe it's just easier
to look at a screen
than in a mirror

it's the conflict of
liking the world better
when I'm drunk
but liking myself more
when I'm sober

how pretty
it would be
to say it was always you

after so many near misses
and almost moments
finally
we found our way back

I think I found comfort
in the possibility
for a few years

maybe it was selfish
to assume
you'd be frozen in time
just like me

can you still love me
after what you've seen

can you still love me
after what you know

can you still love me
even after I hurt you
as badly as he hurt me

there are so many moments
I don't want to lose

but I'm holding on
by the barest edge

and I feel them
slipping
through my fingers
a little more
every day

being stranded
at one in the morning

and asking you
to finish my wine

driving slow
to make the night last
just a little longer

the secrets we whispered
when we drank too much

the looks we shared
across the room

the smile you saved
just for me

I loved it all

but I guess
I forgot
to love

you

do you remember
the way
I used to make you laugh

how you said that I
was your favorite person

my fingers are
aching

my grip is
starting to
fail

are you holding on
from the other side

if I asked
would you

remember

am I trying so hard
to keep something alive
that you just want
to forget

I'm sorry if I'm too late

maybe just being known by you
is enough

it's so rare
to find someone
who sees your heart
for exactly what it is

I don't regret much in my life

everything that's happened
has brought me here

but I wish
I'd realized it
sooner

iii. the empty things

she says hello
but what she really means is
I miss you

he asks how she's been
and she doesn't know
if he actually cares

she says she was thinking of him
but what she really means is
I want you back in my life

he talks for a while
before it goes back to silence

and she assumes that means
he doesn't feel the same way at all

I know what I need to do now

this old life
is like wet clothes
clinging to my skin
and slowing my steps

I've shed the layers before

that past life
is so far in the distance
I can no longer see it
on the horizon

the difference is
this time
I'll be sad to see it go

this goodbye with you
feels jagged and sharp
a piece of glass
beneath bare feet
but you make it look like
watching the sunrise
and sipping your morning coffee

I've been drinking
but I haven't been sleeping

we've been talking
but I haven't been thinking

I've learned
to stop pretending
that things
don't hurt

but I don't know how
to stop loving
who I thought
you were

the perfect cruelty
of wanting the attention
of someone with no intention
of knowing you anymore

I could scream into the void
put on my best lipstick
twist myself
into whatever form
I think you'd like

but it still wouldn't make a difference

but the difference is
not once
does this make me think
I am not enough
anymore

I thought I could
hold on to the past
through you

that if I couldn't go back
at least
having you
would feel the same

but those years are over
and it's time to stop
living inside versions of us
that no longer exist

change pulls at me
like waves on the beach
and the more I try to resist it
the more I'm at risk
of drowning

so I'm letting you go

I can't be
the only one
holding on

I can't be
the only one
keeping us afloat

I can't be
the only one
terrified of starting over

but I will

I've done harder things
than this

I create
chemical reactions
inside perfect strangers
just by spilling ink
onto paper
how can you possibly
tell me
I am not interesting enough
to love

I dance with writer's block
usually at 3 a.m.
when my brain is too tired
to keep out thoughts
I wouldn't usually entertain

it's the impossibility
of my art's worth
being measured
by how many people
have felt what I feel

and the fear
that if no one else has
they'll shake their heads
and close the book

and that will only make me feel
more alone

sometimes I wonder
what my former lovers
and former friends
think when flashes of memory
break free from the recesses of their minds
do they remember
my face
my voice
a version of me
even I cannot remember anymore
do they sit with the memory for a moment
do they laugh and shake their heads
do they even pause
at all

I had a boyfriend
at the time
I published my first book

since I was five
I wanted to be a writer

it was my single biggest goal
to hold a book in my hands
with my name on the cover

it was my greatest life achievement
at the time
something that made
all of the cracks in my bones
feel a little more healed

when a friend had asked
what he thought

he'd waved his hand
and said
that's her thing

and that was all

swatting away my words
like flies on a summer day
with a hand

that had never even bothered
to turn to the first page

the man who whispered
I love you
every night
couldn't have cared less
about what went on in my head

I guess it was easier to love me
without knowing

so now when people tell me
that I'm too picky
or my expectations
are too high

I simply smile
and shrug

because I'd much rather be alone

loving
an outline of me
is not
good enough

I am so tired of being diminished
to a body
an idea
a placeholder
for a man
because he knows he's supposed to have
someone beside him
and anyone will do

you are so
beautiful
and funny
and smart

until

the third date rolls around
and suddenly I'm so confused on why
you're not

naked

now

you are
a tease
and wasting my time
and "not that hot anyway"

and suddenly
the *nice guy*
would very much like
to wield his expectations
like a weapon
to beat you with

suddenly
the drinks

and the door holding
and compliments
were not merely
his character

they were a
carefully orchestrated currency
for which
he now demands
an exchange

an agreement
I'd never signed

an understanding
for one
not two

and it doesn't matter if I go for
the so-called bad boys
or the so-called nice guys

you can say
not all men
all day long

but I'm a woman
who believes in things
she can see

and so far it's been
every man
for me

- to all of the family members who cannot fathom why I am still single

I did not spend
the last twenty-five years of my life
having every bone in my body
broken time and time again
by the impossibilities
of a patriarchal society
just to crush myself even smaller
to cradle a man's ego
like some kind of delicate
breakable thing

a woman's cry for help
is not your opportunity
to show off
that you can yell louder

just for fun

just to see
if you can

deflecting
and changing the subject
instead of listening

does
in fact
make you
one of those men

maybe
not everything
is meant
for you

maybe
instead of
finding a space
clearly built
for someone else
and ripping it apart
piece by piece
until it's something
that makes *you*
more comfortable

you could simply
leave it be
and walk away

they tell me
some day
someone
will come around
and change my mind

as if
the only thing
I could possibly have
to look forward to
in my life

is a man
who would need
to change me
in order
to love me

no matter how nice he is
or how many things
he does right
you are under
no obligation
to love him
and you deserve more
than a lifetime of
trying to convince yourself
that you do

so now you'll write
your songs about me
and I'll write
my poems about you
and maybe that was all
we were ever meant to be

what do you do
moments after you wake
and the last tendrils
of your good dream
fade away
like smoke

how do you feel
the next morning
after a date
on your calendar
you've anticipated for so long
shifts from a circle
to an 'x'

where do you go
once the bucket lists
and the dreams
and the goals
and the aspirations
get ticked off
one by one
until there's nothing left
on the page

how do you cope
with the aftermath
of finality

how do you survive
getting everything
you've ever wanted

the problem is
once other voices get in your head
it's hard to get them out

they've rented a room
tangled the sheets
asked you where to find the ice machine

it used to be just me and myself

and her voice
that sounded like a hug
was the only one that told me
it will be okay
for the longest time

and now there's
him
and you
and them
and that one thing they said
ten years ago
and I can still remember
the exact tone of their voice

I wonder if
I accidentally hit the record button
in my mind
a long time ago

have other people found ways
to not hold on to these things

do the voices ever return their keys?

I know I can do it on my own
I've learned how to mount art on the wall
and fix things when they're broken
how to spend time with myself
and not resent the empty spaces around me

I've spent so many years
learning how to grow and breathe
and treasure this time
instead of waiting for it to pass

and yet
sometimes all I want
is to climb in the passenger seat of my car
because someone else offered to drive

*iv. the things you might
need to hear*

affirmations for the hard days

1. I am good and I am getting better
2. I am growing and I am going at my own pace
3. I am listening and open to the messages the universe has to offer today
4. I am optimistic because today is a new day
5. I do not pretend to be anyone or anything other than who I am
6. I embrace change seamlessly and rise to the new opportunities it presents
7. I have everything I need to succeed
8. I invite abundance and a generous heart
9. I love that I love what I love
10. I release the fears that do not serve me
11. letting go creates space for opportunities to come
12. if not this, then something better
13. my body is worthy and beautiful in this moment and at this size
14. my sensitivity is beautiful
15. my emotions and feelings are valid
16. there is growth in stillness
17. I am infinitely brave
18. I allow myself to receive everything I desire
19. I will be my best self today
20. I am committed to my path
21. I am true to myself
22. I focus on what I can control

23. I am healing more and more every day
24. I am always enough for the right person
25. even in uncertain times, I will handle it
26. I am too determined to be defeated
27. success is defined by my willingness to keep going
28. my goals are attainable and my habits get me there
29. I am capable of achieving my goals
30. I feel strong and well today
31. I am grateful for this moment
32. I am grateful I get to spend my life with myself
33. I love how kind I am to myself
34. my perspective is important
35. I take things one step at a time
36. I am healing from things that have harmed me
37. it's safe for me to let go of what no longer serves me
38. some things take time, and that's okay
39. I am ready for my next step
40. the best is yet to come
41. I trust that I know what is best for me
42. I have the power to change my story
43. my well-being is my top priority
44. I accept myself for who I am today
45. I make myself proud
46. I am powerful and in control of my reality
47. I attract all that is good and meant for me
48. I can do hard things
49. there is space for me to grow

50. my art is important
51. my voice is important
52. *I* am important
53. I am worthy of rest
54. I am grateful for this day and its purpose in my journey
55. I release the need to be perfect in order to feel worthy
56. I am willing to believe that by focusing on feeling good, I make better choices that lead to desired results
57. I believe in myself and my ability to succeed
58. I am grateful for the joy each day brings
59. I want good things for the people I love
60. and I am someone I love
61. I am not other people's opinions of me
62. what I have done today was the best I was able to do today
63. I forgive myself

I am the center
of no one's universe
but my own

no one can be simultaneously
everything I need
and everything they need
all of the time

there's a line between
cutting off people
who don't make an effort
to add to my life

and extending
the kind of grace
I desire
for myself

I find comfort
that the disappointment
is now less crushing
than it was before

and it's not from faith
that someone else
will work out
in the future

it's being okay
even if that never
comes to pass

it's realizing
that where I'm at now
was never where
I thought I'd be

but that isn't necessarily
a bad thing

even if things never change
and the right person never appears
and the picture I held
never materializes

the happiness I feel now

is not inherently lesser
or somehow lacking

the happiness I feel now
could very well be
good enough for me

if you are willing to lose me
I will let you

never again
will I beg someone
to ask me to stay

if you cannot see
the gravity of my absence
it is not my job
to warn you

if you cannot see
the sunlight in my soul
it is not my job
to show you

if you cannot see
the promise
of what you and I
could be

then maybe it was never there at all

how other people
failed to love me
is not my burden to bear

how to convince someone to love you properly

you can't

how to be twenty-five
===

come to peace with knowing
twice as much
and less than half
than you did at eighteen

cherish the promise of lines
whispering at the edges
of your face
proof of a life
experienced vividly

learn new skills
especially
if you're too old for them
and find freedom
in being no good at all

appreciate friendships
for what they are
instead of trying to fit them
all in the same box

retire the self-deprecating humor

speak into the universe
I'm broke
I'm an alcoholic
I'm such a mess

enough times

and it will start to listen

realize no one is paying
nearly as much attention to you
as you think they are

so do the damn thing

I hope you cry
over fictional books
and giggle
at romcoms

I hope you blare
that *girly* band
with the windows down

I hope you wear
your favorite *basic* clothes
because they're comfortable

I hope you don't let the world
beat all of the things you love
out of you

because once you do
it's hard to get them back

there are things I love about myself
little details
habits

the changes in my laugh
depending on how funny something is

the way I'll never get tired
of looking at the moon

how I pick and choose
which lyrics I want to sing in a song

the freckles
on my fingers

the shifting colors
in my eyes

the kind way I speak
to myself and others

one day
someone will notice

and I'll wait until then

as long as I continue
to seek a home
in the hearts of other people
I will continue
to be lost

confidence
and self love
are not things
you have or you don't
something you find or acquire

they're muscles

and like anything
it's about consistency

it's about trying
and then trying again

even on the days
when you feel like
you can't lift the weight

letter #1 to the person I used to be

you're going to feel dumb
foolish

how could you
have been so blind

you're going to cry
and stay up all night

trying to put together pieces
that will never make sense

so you might as well
let your fingers rest

you're going to cringe
and feel shame

like hot water
down your spine

at the things
you can't take back

and the things you wish
you'd left unsaid

you're going to feel unclean
exposed

like he owns parts of you now
and it feels wrong to try to reclaim them

like he's ruined parts of you
for yourself

and now it hurts
to even see your reflection

because all you see
is him looking back

but it doesn't last
it doesn't stay

I'm sorry
for all of the time
you'll have to spend
picking up the pieces

but your body
will shed the skin
he touched
and regenerate itself
until you're nearly brand new

and eventually
there will be a day
when someone asks about him
and it takes you a moment
to remember his name

letter #2 to the person I used to be

I like this new version of myself
but I still miss you sometimes

I'm supposed to be here
now
in this discomfort
in this uncertainty
in this back and forth
of fear and frustration
that I'm wasting time
and I'm in the wrong place

I'm supposed to be here
now
in this doubt
in this imperfection
in this transitionary space
while I come to appreciate
I can't be driving forward
and seeing results
one hundred percent of the time

it is not just
an in between space
a pause
between
the better parts

a skip in a heartbeat
a missed flight
a drive home

this part right here
is its own era

this part right here
has things to show
and things to teach

this part right here
may be quieter
but it
matters
too

because I am on the cusp
of something that is so much more

what next?

Looking for more poetry? Try one of Katie Wismer's other collections:

Poems for the End of the World

The Sweetest Kind of Poison

Thank you for reading! Reviews are one of the best ways to support authors, especially indie authors like myself. If you enjoyed this book, please consider leaving a review on the site where you got it. It really helps the books out, and I appreciate it so much!

sign up for my author newsletter

Sign up for Katie Wismer's newsletter to receive exclusive content and be the first to learn about new releases, book sales, events, and other news! Signed paperbacks can also be found on her site.

www.katiewismer.com

about the author

Katie Wismer is a freelance editor and author of romance (sometimes contemporary, sometimes paranormal) and poetry books.

Be the first to know about upcoming projects, exclusive content, and more by signing up for her newsletter at katiewismer.com or checking out her exclusive videos at patreon.com/katiewismer.

When she's not reading, writing, or wrangling her two perfect cats, you can find her on her YouTube channel Katesbookdate.

patreon.com/katiewismer
instagram.com/katesbookdate
goodreads.com/katesbookdate
bookbub.com/authors/katie-wismer
facebook.com/authorkatiewismer
amazon.com/author/katiewismer
twitter.com/katesbookdate